Love Your Books *by Angie Rowe*

ILLUSTRATED BY
Natalia Rowe

DESIGNED BY
Dan Clarke - Telford Repro

"For all the people who dedicate their time helping animals to live a wonderful life" 🐾

Angela Rowe
angie.rowe@loveyour-books.com

www.loveyour-books.com

Love Your Budgie

ISBN 978-1-9163572-2-8

Love Your Books

by Angie Rowe

Love your Cat

Love your Hamster

Love your Rabbit

Love your Horse

Love your Fish

Love your Dog

To Parents, Carers & Teachers

These 'Love Your' Books are to help bring out empathy, compassion and kindness within your child and their natural loving nature to shine through.

To love all animals domestic and wild, whether big or small is one of the best traits to have.

Cruelty should **NEVER** belong in a childs heart.

Your Budgie needs SEED

Without WATER

Your Budgie needs Big CAGE and COVER

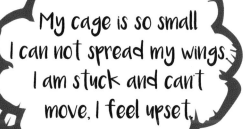

Your Budgie needs TOYS

Without TOYS

Without A BIRD BATH

DON'T

- **LEAVE CAGE DIRTY**

- **LEAVE CAGE NEAR A WINDOW**

- **LEAVE CAGE NEAR LOUD TV OR SPEAKERS**

- **LEAVE YOUR BUDGIE TO FLY FREELY UNATTENDED**

IT IS CRUEL

DO

- **VARY YOUR BUDGIES DIET**

- **GIVE FRESH WATER DAILY**

- **GIVE AFFECTION**

- **GIVE YOUR BUDGIE A MIRROR**

REMEMBER
YOUR BUDGIE LOVES
YOU VERY MUCH

In a world where you can be anything
BE KIND

Colour me correctly

Colour me
CRAZY

Printed in Great Britain
by Amazon

62965967R00015